MISSILES
AND
ROCKETS

MARK DARTFORD

angus

This edition published in 2004 by Angus Books
12 Ravensbury Terrace
London
SW18 4RL

ISBN 1-904594-38-7

The Brown Reference Group plc
8 Chapel Place
Rivington Street
London
EC2A 3DQ

Production by Omnipress,
Eastbourne, UK
Printed and bound in Dubai

This book uses black and yellow chevrons as a decorative element on some headers. They do not point to other elements on the page.

Contents

Introduction

On the deck of a warship, a hatch flips open. An object shoots out in a burst of flame and smoke. It curves toward the horizon and is soon gone, leaving a **vapour trail**. Minutes later, the object swoops down low on course for the target. A sea-launched Tomahawk cruise missile heads toward its mark.

UP AND AWAY

A Tomahawk cruise missile begins its journey from the deck of a U.S. Navy guided missile destroyer. Cruise missiles can carry nuclear or old-style **warheads**. They can fly close to the surface, where they are hard to detect.

>> **vapour trail** = a white trail left by a missile or aircraft in the sky

Missiles of All Kinds

Most people think of missiles as weapons of modern warfare. However, missiles and projectiles have existed for a long time. Projectiles are objects that are thrown toward an enemy by force. They include arrows, spears, bullets or shells. Missiles travel using their own power.

EARLY MISSILES

Attackers throw barrels of burning tar onto a fort. Sometimes attackers dumped dead animals onto forts. The rotting animals could spread disease among the defenders.

ANTHEM

"...And the rocket's red glare, the bombs bursting in air, Gave proof through the night that our flag was still there...."

"Star Spangled Banner," Francis Scott Key, Battle of Baltimore eyewitness, 1814

RED GLARE

Rockets are launched in the early 1800s. The British used rockets against U.S. defenders at the Battle of Baltimore during the War of 1812 (1812–1815). The event is remembered in "The Star-Spangled Banner," the national anthem of the United States.

World War II

Modern missile technology had its origins in World War II (1939–1945). German scientists built the first cruise and **ballistic missiles.** In 1944 the Germans launched V-1 flying bombs and V-2 rockets against targets in Europe and Britain.

FIRST CRUISE

A German V-1 falls on London, England. V-1s were programmed to fly to their targets, like unmanned aeroplanes. They were powered by simple **ramjet** motors. Their warheads exploded when they hit the ground.
V-1s were the first cruise missiles but they were not very accurate. The Germans launched about 8,000 V-1s against London. Fewer than 2,000 actually hit the city.

FIRST BALLISTIC MISSILE

V-2s were the first ballistic missiles. The Germans set off V-2 rockets from northwestern Europe. Most were aimed at London. They reached a height of 65 miles and a speed of 3,500 miles per hour. The V-2s fell without warning on the city. They carried 2,200 pounds of high explosives.

ROCKET MAN

Wernher von Braun (with bandaged arm) was the inventor of the V-2 rocket. He surrendered to the Allies in 1945. Von Braun was more interested in building moon rockets than missiles. After the war, he worked in the United States. He became a founder of the National Aeronautics and Space Administration (NASA).

>> **ramjet** – a simple jet engine that has no turbine blades

Missile Race

To end World War II, the United States dropped **atom bombs** on the Japanese cities of Hiroshima and Nagasaki. The bombs caused massive damage. The world's leading nations began to develop missiles that could carry these powerful weapons of mass destruction.

BALLISTIC MISSILES

A Minuteman III long-range ballistic missile is launched in California. Ballistic missiles are programmed before launch. They travel far above Earth before falling onto their targets. Ballistic missiles can be either ground-launched **intercontinental** ballistic missiles (ICBMs) or submarine-launched ballistic missiles (SLBMs)

CRUISE MISSILES

A U.S. Tomahawk cruise missile in flight. Cruise missiles can be launched from aeroplanes or ships or from the ground. They carry their own navigational equipment. Cruise missiles fly at low level. This makes them difficult to find.

BATTLEFIELD MISSILES

Battlefield missiles are often launched from vehicles that can be moved around in the battle zone. Warships can also launch these short-range missiles.

The Missile's Job

Missiles have either a tactical (battlefield) or a strategic (political) role. Tactical missiles are designed to attack enemy vehicles, aircraft, ships or troops. Strategic missiles often carry weapons of mass destruction. Their main job is to convince an enemy not to attack in the first place because of the threat of a powerful response.

Tactical Missiles

Aeroplanes, ships, armoured vehicles and infantry troops can all have tactical missiles for attack or defence.

AIRCRAFT MISSILES

An F16 Fighting Falcon launches one of its wingtip Sidewinder air-to-air missiles. Aeroplanes and helicopters carry missiles for strike missions, air-to-air combat and defence.

SHIP MISSILES

A British frigate launches a Harpoon surface-to-surface missile. The Harpoon is guided by **radar.** It flies close to the surface to avoid being found by the enemy. Sea-launched missiles have replaced the artillery (big guns) of earlier warships.

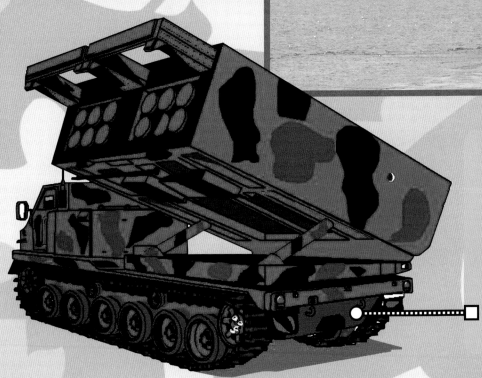

AFV MISSILES

The U.S. Army has Multiple Launch Rocket System (MLRS) vehicles. An MLRS can fire up to six missiles at a time. It can move rapidly around the battlefield. This makes it difficult for the enemy to hit. Battlefield missiles can hit targets like artillery guns, but they are more accurate and easier to move.

INFANTRY MISSILES

A U.S. Marine fires an M47 Dragon wire-guided anti-tank missile. The missile's **guide wire** helps him pinpoint the target. Ground forces are equipped with small, handheld missiles. These can be used against armoured vehicles or aircraft.

>> **guide wire** – a wire carrying control signals from the firer to the missile **11**

Strategic Missiles

Strategic missiles are the big hitters. They can travel very long distances and arrive with little or no warning. They can carry nuclear warheads and can threaten whole cities and countries. Strategic missiles have been in existence since the middle 1900s.

ALWAYS READY

During a test launch, protective heat tiles fall away from a Peacekeeper ICBM. Such weapons have not been used in war. But the rockets and their systems are often tested. They need to be ready for any sudden threat. The tests are carried out using only small amounts of explosives or none at all.

STRATEGY AT SEA

A Trident SLBM breaks the water from a U.S. Navy nuclear-powered submarine. The missile is launched while the submarine is underwater. It is almost impossible to find. Nuclear-powered submarines can remain underwater for many months. They can strike at any target in the world from any ocean without being seen.

>> **re-entry** = when a missile passes from space back into Earth's atmosphere

ALL IN ONE

A timed photograph shows the path of warheads from a Peacekeeper ICBM. Ballistic missiles are usually fitted with multiple independently targetable **re-entry** vehicles (MIRVs). These warheads carry **submunitions** that spread out when the missile reaches its target area. This allows the missiles to strike at several places at once.

Power and Politics

Strategic missiles are important political tools. Each nation that has strategic missile weapons can put political pressure on its enemies. But all opponents know that any attack will mean their own destruction in a counterattack. This is sometimes called Mutually Assured Destruction (MAD).

Toward a Safer World

Communism in the Soviet Union and its European allies collapsed at the end of the 1980s. The United States and Russia (which succeeded the Soviet Union) began talks to reduce the number of ballistic missiles both sides had.

START AND SALT

Representatives from the United States and Russia meet in Vienna in 1998 to agree on a programme of reducing nuclear weapons. These discussions were known as the Strategic Arms Limitation Talks (SALT). They followed an agreement signed between the United States and Russia in 1993 called the Strategic Arms Reduction Treaty (START). This meant cutting back on both ground- and submarine-launched ballistic missiles.

HOMEWARD BOUND

A U.S. Air Force C141 Starlifter carries missiles away from an airbase in Europe in the late 1980s. The missiles are being flown back to the United States. The **Cold War** was coming to an end. Relations between the Soviet Union and the United States were improving. It no longer seemed necessary to have so many strategic weapons in Europe.

>> **Cold War** = a period of political and military tension but not warfare

How Missiles Work

Modern missiles are far more effective than the simple rockets developed in World War II. Computers, radar, **infrared** and satellite technology have all made missiles more accurate and deadly.

Fire-and-Forget

AIR TO AIR

A closeup shows a Sidewinder air **interception** missile attached to an aircraft's wingtip. Once it is launched, the Sidewinder locks on to its target. It uses infrared heat-seeking sensors to find the enemy. Missiles like the Sidewinder find their targets using their own guidance systems. They are sometimes called fire-and-forget missiles. They allow the crew to focus on their job, while the missile does its job.

>> **infrared** = relating to heat put out by an aircraft engine

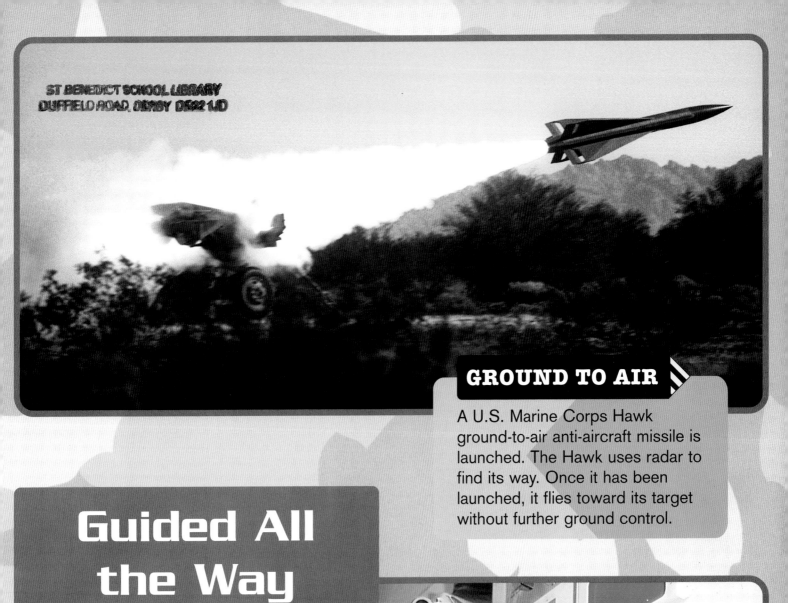

GROUND TO AIR

A U.S. Marine Corps Hawk ground-to-air anti-aircraft missile is launched. The Hawk uses radar to find its way. Once it has been launched, it flies toward its target without further ground control.

Guided All the Way

GENTLE TOUCH

A Navy technician makes careful changes to the delicate guidance controls of a Sea Sparrow missile. The controls must be checked often to make sure the system works properly.

How Missiles Work

Rocket science is used for both military and nonmilitary purposes. The technology required to send a rocket into space is a lot like the technology needed to send a ballistic missile toward a target.

Space Know-How

SHARED TECHNOLOGY

A space probe takes off from a U.S. Air Force Delta rocket. Much of the science developed to make rockets for space exploration has also been used for missile design. Strategic missiles like the Trident, the Minuteman, and the Peacekeeper have systems that are also used in NASA's Titan, Mercury and Atlas spacecraft.

TACTICAL NUCLEAR

A U.S. Army Pershing II tactical nuclear missile. Missiles like the Pershing are smaller than the long-range strategic nuclear weapons of mass destruction. But they are bigger and much more powerful than non-nuclear battlefield missiles. They can destroy anything within about a mile of their **blast point.**

Inside a Missile

TRIDENT

This illustration shows the inside of a Trident II submarine-launched intercontinental ballistic missile. It is a three-stage rocket. Its MIRVs are located in the top section all around the third stage motor.

aerospike

nose fairing/cap

payload

third stage motor

post-boost control system

equipment section

second stage motor

inter-stage

first stage motor

Missiles and Rockets

Missiles range in size from small shoulder-fired weapons to huge strategic missiles. Small missiles have just enough explosives to damage an AFV. The big missiles can destroy whole cities.

PEACEKEEPER II

The Peacekeeper II ICBM is the most advanced intercontinental ballistic missile in the world. It has up to ten accurate **re-entry vehicles.** As part of START, the Peacekeeper II missile is being taken out of the national defence programme. ICBMs have **inertial guidance** systems.

Details:
Function: ground-launched ICBM
Length: 71 ft.
Weight: 195,000 lbs.
Diameter: 7 ft. 8 in.
Range: over 6,000 miles
Max Speed: 15,000 mph
Warhead: 10 x re-entry vehicles

MINUTEMAN III

A Minuteman III missile blasts off across the Pacific. Five hundred Minuteman missiles are based in silos across the north central United States. They are the nation's main deterrent against nuclear attack. Minuteman missiles have been in operation since the 1960s. They have been updated over the years.

Details:
Function: ground-launched ICBM
Length: 59 ft. 10 in.
Weight: 79,432 lbs.
Diameter: 5 ft. 6 in.
Range: over 6,000 miles
Max Speed: 15,000 mph
Warhead: 1 x re-entry vehicle

TRIDENT II

Underwater launch of a Trident submarine missile. Trident II is a changing member of the U.S. Navy's ballistic missile programme. The programme began in the 1950s with the submarine-launched Polaris missile. It was followed by the Poseidon and then by the Trident I. Submarine-launched missiles are very powerful deterrents. They can be launched underwater from any ocean.

Details:
Function: submarine-launched ICBM
Length: 44 ft.
Weight: 130,000 lbs.
Diameter: 6 ft. 2 in.
Range: over 4,500 miles
Max Speed: 13,500 mph
Warhead: 1 x manoeuvreable re-entry
    vehicle

Missiles and Rockets

Ground missiles do a job similar to artillery. Missiles are more accurate than shells fired from big guns. Ground missiles are used against troops, buildings, AFVs and aircraft.

MLRS

A U.S. Army launch vehicle prepares to fire. The M26 MLRS is a short-range battlefield weapon. It can direct a barrage of fire against targets in a short space of time. MLRS is highly mobile and was a great success during the Gulf War in 1991.

Details:
Function: tactical rocket artillery
Length: 13 ft. (rocket)
Weight: 5,000 lbs.
Diameter: 8.8 in.
Range: 4 miles
Max Speed: variable, **subsonic**
Warhead: 1 x timed **fragmentation burst**

JAVELIN

U.S. Marines fire a Javelin anti-tank missile. The Javelin is a portable, fire-and-forget weapon. It is replacing the Dragon anti-tank shoulder-launched missile in the U.S. Army and the Marine Corps. The Javelin is guided by infrared.

Details:
Function: individual anti-tank missile
Length: 5 ft. 8 in.
Weight: 49.5 lbs.
Diameter: 5 in.
Range: 1.5 miles
Max Speed: variable, subsonic
Warhead: high explosive

RAPIER

The Rapier is a mobile anti-aircraft missile system developed in Britain. Many countries in Europe and Asia use the radar-guided Rapier. It can defend an area up to ten miles wide and up to three miles high.

Details:
Function: anti-aircraft missile
Length: 7 ft. 6 in.
Weight: 92.4 lbs.
Diameter: 5 in.
Range: 5 miles
Max Speed: Mach 2.5
Warhead: high explosive

>> **fragmentation burst** = pieces of jagged metal that rip into armour

Missiles and Rockets

Sea-launched missiles are used for both defence and attack. They are aimed at other ships or submarines or at attacking aircraft. Some ships also carry land-attack missiles, such as the Tomahawk cruise missile.

SEA SPARROW

The Sea Sparrow RIM7 anti-aircraft missile works well against both aircraft and missile attack. Sea Sparrow is in use with the U.S. Navy and with other countries. The missile is guided by radar.

Details:
Function: surface-to-air aerial defence
Length: 12 ft.
Weight: 500 lbs.
Diameter: 8 in.
Range: up to 50 miles
Max Speed: 2,660 mph
Warhead: fragmentation warhead

>> **penetration** – a warhead that bores through armour before exploding

HARPOON

A radar-guided RGM84 Harpoon surface-to-surface missile bursts from the U.S. Navy cruiser USS *Leahy.* The Harpoon was developed especially for attacking ships. It can be launched from other ships, from submarines or from aircraft.

Details:
Function: maritime ship attack
Length: 15 ft.
Weight: 1,470 lbs.
Diameter: 13.5 in.
Range: more than 60 miles
Max Speed: 500 mph
Warhead: **penetration** high explosive

TOMAHAWK

A BGM109 Tomahawk cruise missile is launched from the deck of the aircraft carrier USS *La Jolla* in 1991. These land-attack weapons are very accurate. Some even flew along the streets of Iraq's capital city of Baghdad to find their targets.

Details:
Function: long-range land attack
Length: 18 ft. 3 in.
Weight: 2,650 lbs.
Diameter: 20.4 in.
Range: 700 mi.
Max Speed: 550 mph
Warhead: high explosive, **bomblets** or nuclear

Missiles and Rockets

aUnlike ground- or ship-launched missiles, aircraft missiles are already travelling at high speed before they are released. This makes them even more effective and harder to attack.

SIDEWINDER

A U.S. Air Force F22 Raptor fires its Sidewinder missile. The AIM9 Sidewinder is a **supersonic,** heat-seeking, air-to-air missile carried by fighter aircraft. It has been in service with U.S. forces and other countries around the world for nearly half a century. Ongoing improvements have kept the Sidewinder at the top of missile technology.

Details:
Function: air-to-air attack
Length: 9 ft. 5 in.
Weight: 190 lbs.
Diameter: 5 in.
Range: up to 18 miles
Max Speed: Mach 2.5
Warhead: fragmentation high explosive

MAVERICK

A U.S. Air Force F16 Fighting Falcon fires a Maverick missile. The Maverick AGM65 is a close-range air-to-ground missile. It is used mostly to support ground actions. Guided either by radar or by laser, it is effective against many different types of targets.

Details:
Function: air-to-surface ground attack
Length: 8 ft. 2 in.
Weight: up to 670 lbs.
Diameter: 12 in.
Range: up to 18 miles
Max Speed: 720 mph
Warhead: penetration high explosive

A U.S. Navy SH60 helicopter fires a Penguin missile. The AGM119 Penguin missile is made in Norway. It is the only helicopter air-to-surface anti-ship missile used by the U.S. Navy.

Details:
Function: helicopter anti-ship missile
Length: 10 ft. 3 in.
Weight: 847 lbs.
Diameter: 11.2 in.
Range: up to 3 miles
Max Speed: Mach 1.2
Warhead: **armour-piercing** high explosive

Missiles of the Future

The next generation of missiles will be more powerful and more accurate. They will require less maintenance and human control. World peace negotiations focus on reducing weapons of mass destruction. As a result, there will be fewer ICBMs but more specialized tactical weapons.

RISING STANDARD

Shrouded in smoke and flame, an experimental Standard III missile is launched from the cruiser USS *Lake Erie*. The Standard III will attack approaching ICBMs. It will be part of the Star Wars defence programme.

METEOR

A Swedish air force Saab Gripen launches a long-range Meteor missile. The Meteor is being developed by six countries. It will be an all-weather, **beyond-visual-range** missile. Its high-tech guidance systems will overcome ECM.

TACTICAL TOMAHAWK

A Tactical Tomahawk is launched at a U.S. Navy test site. The new generation of Tomahawk cruise missiles will have pinpoint accuracy. It will also be possible to **re-program** the Tactical Tomahawk in flight to change targets. It will be able to delay over a target before striking so it can hit at the most effective moment. It will be launched from ships and submarines.

Missiles of the Future

The most dangerous missiles travel mostly through space. Space technology is a vital part of the Star Wars programme. It aims to put enemy missiles out of action long before they can get within striking distance.

HIGH FLIGHT

An F15 Eagle satellite buster pushes up through the **stratosphere.** High-altitude aeroplanes can fly to the edge of space. They can launch missiles that will destroy enemy communications and control satellites.

Satellite Killers

HIGH-ENERGY LASER

The High-Energy Laser (HEL) is another laser satellite programme. It is under development in the United States as part of the Star Wars programme.